SCULPTING SPACE

House Design
BARRY A. BERKUS

SCULPTING SPACE

House Design
BARRY A. BERKUS

10

First published in Australia in 2002 by
The Images Publishing Group Pty Ltd
ABN 89 059 734 431
6 Bastow Place, Mulgrave, Victoria, 3170, Australia
Telephone +613 9561 5544 Facsimile +613 9561 4860
Email books@images.com.au
Website www.imagespublishinggroup.com

National Library of Australia
Cataloguing-in-Publication data

Berkus, Barry A.
Sculpting space.

ISBN 1 86470 088 2.

1. Berkus, Barry A. 2. Architecture, Domestic - United States.
3. Architecture, Domestic - 20th century. I. Title.
(Series : House design ; no. 10).

728.0973

Final production by The Graphic Image Studio Pty Ltd, Melbourne
Film by Mission Productions
Printed by Sing Cheong Printing Co. Ltd. Hong Kong.

dedication

To my late wife Gail Berkus, may you continue to make paper from clouds.

To our children, Jeff, Carey, and Steven, their spouses and children.

To my Mom, always an inspiration.

To Pat Moser, my long-time assistant and friend.

To the clients, architects, and builders who were instrumental in making these buildings come to life.

table of contents

acknowledgments

This book would not have taken flight without The Images Publishing Group, which asked me to be a part of this outstanding series shortly after publishing my first book, *Architecture, Art, Parallels, Connections*. I am inspired by their continued perseverance and dedication to the field of architecture.

I would like to extend thanks to: Kristin Anderson and Lauren DeChant for their editorial and creative input, and contributions to layout and design; Ben Petit for proofreading and editing with such objectivity; Jo Cahow for a second read; and Andy Goldsworthy for his continued inspiration and words of encouragement.

Few of us in the field of architecture create without the substantial involvement of a team that assists in many phases of design and documentation of the buildings. In my 40 years of architectural practice, it would be impossible to name all the architects and designers who have played a role in the designs featured in this book. With that in mind, I would like to extend thanks to all who have contributed to my projects over the years.

from the author

While writing this book I was once again reminded of the kinship between creating architecture and art. Memories of time spent with Andy Goldsworthy came to mind. In 1992, I had the opportunity to watch Andy at work as he created a project that my wife Gail and I commissioned in Santa Barbara, California.

His ability to transform natural materials into a sculpted art form will forever live in my mind as magical. Andy is able to mold wood, stone, sand, and ice into objects with thought and volume much like architectural ventures.

After witnessing his creative process, I realized we share quintessential similarities in the way we approach our crafts, particularly our perceptions of sculpted forms and space.

I sent the manuscript for this book to Andy and asked if he would write a brief foreword. I am honored and grateful that he contributed the following words.

Barry Berkus
Santa Barbara, California

foreword

I first met Barry with his wife Gail at their home in Santa Barbara, California in 1992, at a time when my work was largely unknown on the west coast. Cheryl Haines, the owner of Haines Gallery in San Francisco, organized my visit. She had struggled to find people to host and fund a period of my work that would form the basis of an exhibition at her gallery.

Mr. and Mrs. Berkus embraced my project with a real leap of faith, curiosity and open-mindedness—all qualities that can be recognized in the way Barry approaches architecture.

Barry puts a lot of importance on listening, looking, and learning in his work. Within minutes of being introduced to him, I was asked many searching questions about my art, my creative process, and my inspirations. I have not been a client of Barry's, but I could imagine from my first meeting that anyone asking for a Berkus-designed house would be

subjected to a similarly intense series of questions about their expectations and dreams. He does not see the client as an opposition to ideas but as an opportunity to provoke new architectural responses.

Barry is one of only a few architects I have met who embraces contemporary art, and my visit to Santa Barbara was a result of that interest. I remember well his collection of art, and discussing an idea he had for a book about the relationship between architecture and art. It was exciting to see these ideas turn into concrete form when *Architecture, Art, Parallels, Connections* was published in 2000.

Sculpting Space is an intensely personal, direct, and clear explanation of not so much how, but why the houses described in this book came into existence. Barry's notes and comments are an insight into the processes that take place in the realization of a design, and a reflection of the creativity that can be expressed by the artisan's hand.

Andy Goldsworthy
February 2002

"All forms are to be found in nature, and there are many qualities within any material. By exploring them, I hope to understand the whole. My work needs to include the loose and distorted within the nature of the material as well as the tight and regular."

Andy Goldsworthy

introduction

Sculpting Space presents and interprets a pictorial narrative that I see as integral to sculpting architectural form around human activity. As an architect, I sculpt space by defining negative and positive space into organic and geometric planes much like a sculptor creating fine art. But a sculptor is often free to develop art as a pure expression of creativity, molding his or her thoughts into three dimensions. The architect is responsible to the voice of the inhabitants, and the dimensional form that emerges represents a collaboration of thought.

1

In site-specific work, I believe a sculptor faces challenges similar to those of an architect. Issues raised by the surrounding physical and cultural environment must be considered in conjunction with the artist's will. I have spent my career as an architect collaborating with clients to define site-specific spaces that call to action the spirit of those within.

2

3

1   Work in progress by Andy Goldsworthy, Santa Barbara, California
2   Framework of Via Vistosa, Santa Barbara, California
3   Sculpture by Mark DiSuvero

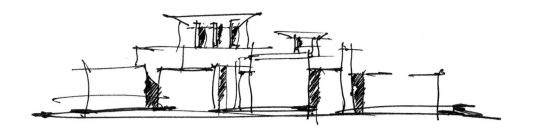

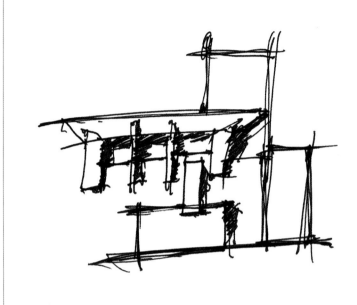

elieve there is a science to determining proportion and scale when translating chitectural concepts into built form. It is based on accommodating and couraging movement of the inhabitants, as well as creating a spatial lationship between the human and the physical space. The control of light and adow and the awareness of daily paths traveled within a space is part of the ence explored in the process of design.

I have traveled through life, I have amassed a collection of physical and visual emories. To those memories, I have added a deep appreciation for the arts, in rticular the abstract, as a conveyance of inspiration. I believe the fusion of ese ideas has endowed me with a dimension of thought that frees me from nvention. It offers a vast canvas on which to express ideas and designs.

y hope is that those who spend time with this work will be inspired to search r a sculpted form that in turn inspires their spirit.

Yagoda Residence, Scottsdale, Arizona
Church window, Puglia, Italy

6

One of the most memorable days in my life was walking through the Storm King Sculpture Park in Mountainville, New York on a cold windy day. I watched the yellow leaves of autumn move freely through the large-scale sculpture, which to me became architecture standing within a garden. The manner in which the sculpture compels one to engage—guiding the eye and physical movements through and around its surfaces—is akin to the emotion the architect attempts to provoke through a structure.

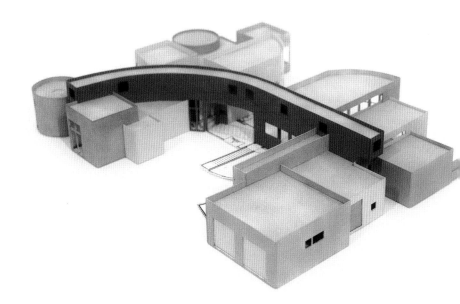

7

6   Storm King Sculpture Park, Mountainville, New York
7   Model of private residence, Palm Desert, California
8   Schoor Pool House, Colt's Neck, New Jersey

8

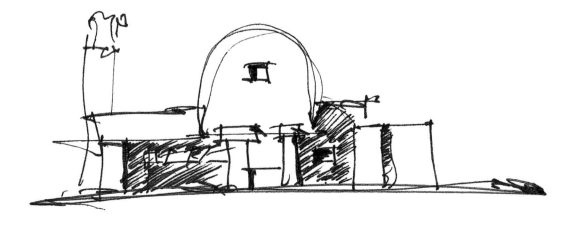

connecting the old to the new

9

One of the great challenges of architecture is understanding the significance of the architectural past within a contemporary context. The more mature I become, the more I appreciate the dialogues of the past that have created a marriage of thought between land and structure in the communities of old.

The great hill towns in Europe and the farm and manor houses found in the surrounding fields are placeholders of past expressions that provide examples of great historical reference, stimulating thought about the origins of shape and form.

By wandering through these hill towns and plains and viewing these structures with an inquisitive eye, these structural forms and expressions become indelible parts of my knowledge base. The more worldly my travel experience, the broader my reservoir of knowledge becomes.

There are times when I will take specific trips to follow an architect's work—Bofil's work in Spain, Corbusier's work in France, Paladio's in Italy, etc. In my attempt to understand the motivation behind their creations, I absorb additional ideas about the design process. I have found that a better understanding of the old can often provide innovative standards for contemporary design.

9   Positano, Italy
10 Weekley Residence, Carmel, California
11 Interior, Terner Residence, Pacific Palisades, California
12 Entry, custom residence, Palm Desert, California

10

ding from the inside out

Many architects design buildings from the outside in. The external geometry tends to define the internal space. In my approach to sculpting space, the structures are designed with the interests and expressions of the clients as well as the architect's intuition. When I begin the design of a structure, I mold these ideas and perceptions into a physical form.

During this process of sculpting space, I mold the skeletal form of the house or building. Dialogue emerges as components start to grow within the building, and I begin to understand the connections and space. Many times, junctions are discovered that create pleasant surprises.

The artistic process of sculpting space gives each room in a house its own personality, destination, and character.

A niche may create a feeling of comfort or security, whereas an open, grander space may offer a different experience. People need freedom to change their environment; this prevents a structure from becoming static. I have found that organic shape tends to fit the needs of a human being more comfortably than rigid geometry. Rooms sculpted in an organic shape may be catalysts to thought or conversation not touched upon in a geometric form, encompassing activity rather than acting as a rigid canister. I believe it is always important to consider the human being while shaping their environment. In order to achieve this goal, the architect–client relationship becomes a formative part of the process.

Throughout my career, I have been engaged in personal exchanges between client and architect that often evolve into long-term relationships. One of the most important aspects of this relationship is the architect's ability to listen to the client's needs. Through open discussion about the client's needs and desires, new ideas emerge for both the client and architect. Sculpting of space speaks to this dialogue, and the resulting structure represents a true collaboration of both parties.

Opposite
Skylit library silo, Via Vistosa, Santa Barbara, California

14

When first studying architecture as a student, one thinks of creating an architectural legacy. I have found that the process of designing a home gives one the opportunity to interact with the human spirit at a level much more personal than that experienced in designing a public building or monument. The architectural legacy created in this personal sphere may very well be that of the family as well as the structure. My experiences and studies become a multi-faceted lens through which I am able to recognize and interpret the desires of my clients, a task I find tremendously rewarding.

In this book, you will discover a broad palette of architectural styles at work. Each style describes or elaborates upon the process of sculpting space as a unique portrait of the architectural interpretation of the client's needs through my eyes.

14   Model, Ortega Ridge Residence,
     Summerland, California
Opposite
     The Tokyo City Hall Complex
     designed by Kenzo Tange

the process begins...defining the vision

Prior to the design of each home, the clients are asked to write a program or scenario of what this building will mean to them and the goals it may achieve for the individual or family. The voices of all are heard in this storytelling process. Below are excerpts from client programs.

"The idea of building our own house has always been a dream for us, but a dream based more in fantasy than reality, thus I have not spent years planning what I'd have in my dream house. Now that the dream is becoming a reality, I have become completely enamored with the site we are purchasing and of the idea of creating a home that will be uniquely ours. The details of what that design means are just beginning to take form."

"I've been drawn to homes with heart, soul, and hum that absolutely reflected and related to the people occupied them. Like a fingerprint, it should be one kind…"

"So this home has to be comfortable—has to make us all feel that we belong…enable us to relax and enjoy each other's company, conversation, ideas, problems, and dreams. It should create an atmosphere that makes it easy to open up and communicate. I hope it doesn't sound like we want to live in a log cabin with an outhouse down wind; beauty is very important, we want great design, sensuous materials, fabulous workmanship, wonderful art, and wit. It must fit into the surroundings—be a part of the site—enhance not overwhelm."

1

"Flow of house and continuity of design is very important—we do not want to walk through a room to get to a room…the home must have a warm feeling—we love contemporary architecture, but cold sharp angles do not suit us."

2

"Here nature and stability, sky and shelter blend in a home that opens the world to us and becomes the nourishing environment of our future."

"I've been drawn to homes with heart, soul, and humility that absolutely reflected and related to the people who occupied them. Like a fingerprint, it should be one of a kind…it is not a tool to impress, but one to embrace, comfort, stimulate, etc. It is home. It is us. We want it [our home] to grow up and settle down, to be so comfortable in all its attributes that it will have no need to impress. Then it can make the world a better place for its being there and improve upon every life it touches."

"Light. We must have light. We hate dark, dreary houses, which can only be inhabited by moles or monks. Therefore, we loved the large windows in the model home. And we also love floor-to-ceiling windows and French doors…we like the feeling of space yet at the same time we do like private areas. I know this sounds contradictory, but somehow we felt that your "model" home captured that…I have a particular fondness for rooms which are virtually surrounded by light and have a solarium effect. If it is humanly possible for my office to capture this feeling, I would worship at your shrine and throw rose petals in your path."

"As we dream of the house it is warm and protective, yet as open to nature as if it had neither walls nor roof…it is as familiar as home and as mysterious as paradise. The house is the outer envelope of our being, the place and time where we will perfect ourselves into the people we will become."

1   Model of Henry Residence
2   Model of Doumani Residence

woodleigh residence

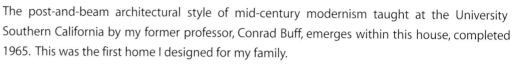

1965 | pasadena, california

The post-and-beam architectural style of mid-century modernism taught at the University Southern California by my former professor, Conrad Buff, emerges within this house, completed 1965. This was the first home I designed for my family.

Concrete columns and timber trusses with infill glass curtain walls create a canister that illuminated by natural light by day. At night, lit from within, the house appears as a lantern amid the gardens. The shifting light from daybreak to sunset moves through the wide expanses of gla creating dynamic forms and climactic shifts.

I have fond memories of my children's friends visiting and spending time in our home, whic seemingly became a magnet for inquisitive young minds. Spatial relationships were sculpted to off an open diagram for passive and active events, providing areas where human interaction flowe through the canister, animating the space, as well as secluded enclaves for individuals or the famil

1

blic and social spaces were
cated on the first floor; the
pper level comprised a library
nd master bedroom. The
ildren had their own wing,
ving them territorial
mperative within the main
ouse. A womb-like, organic
ick structure punctuated the
ter edges, becoming a
eparture from the open
olumes of the two-story
ructure.

Post-and-beam influences are
clearly seen in the Woodleigh
home
A curved brick element penetrates
the open interior space frame
View of suspended library above
the main floor

3

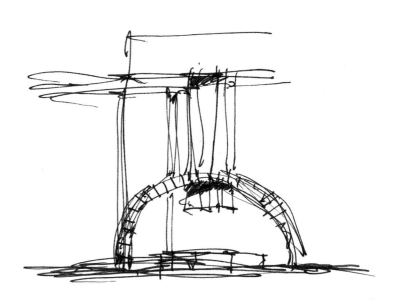

2

4

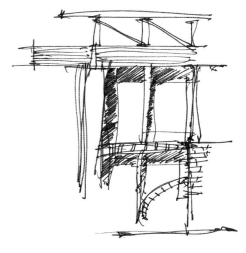

4 Concrete columns, post-and-beam, and timber trusses with infill glass curtain walls create a canister that intensely illuminates the interior space during the day. At night, the house appears as a lantern within its surrounding gardens

5 The living room contains a walk-through fireplace

open to below

library

open to below

sitting
room

master
bedroom

via vistosa

1976 | santa barbara, california

I consider the second home I designed for my family to be the beginning of an organic series, including Via Abrigada and the Westen Residence featured in this book, that combines the more rigid post-and-beam style of architecture with free sculptural shapes. In the process of experimenting with these free shapes, I found myself returning to visions of nature and foregoing the sometimes predictable linear patterns found in modernist design.

Composers of jazz and other experimental music often venture outside defined territory by taking creative license to contrast sounds and rhythms that would traditionally be perceived as incongruous. The composition that emerges in this process may very well establish a new relationship between sound and rhythm, creating resolution where chaos previously existed. Similarly, by playing with combinations of shapes and forms not usually paired in architectural design, I began freeing myself from past influences. In this process, I attempted to tame the chaotic nature of colliding geometry by interweaving organic and geometric shapes in the Via Vistosa residence, introducing a new composition of form.

1   Living room
2   View of Via Vistosa from backyard

1

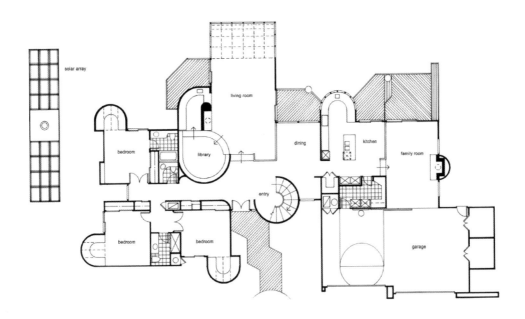

solar array

bedroom

library

living room

dining

kitchen

family room

entry

bedroom

bedroom

garage

In keeping with this concept of redefining connections of shapes and form, I created a sculptured living environment that departed from traditional rectangular room relationships. Volume and light were introduced into the center of the dwelling through sky-lit funnels, creating silos over the stair and library that recalled the silo forms found in rural farmhouses.

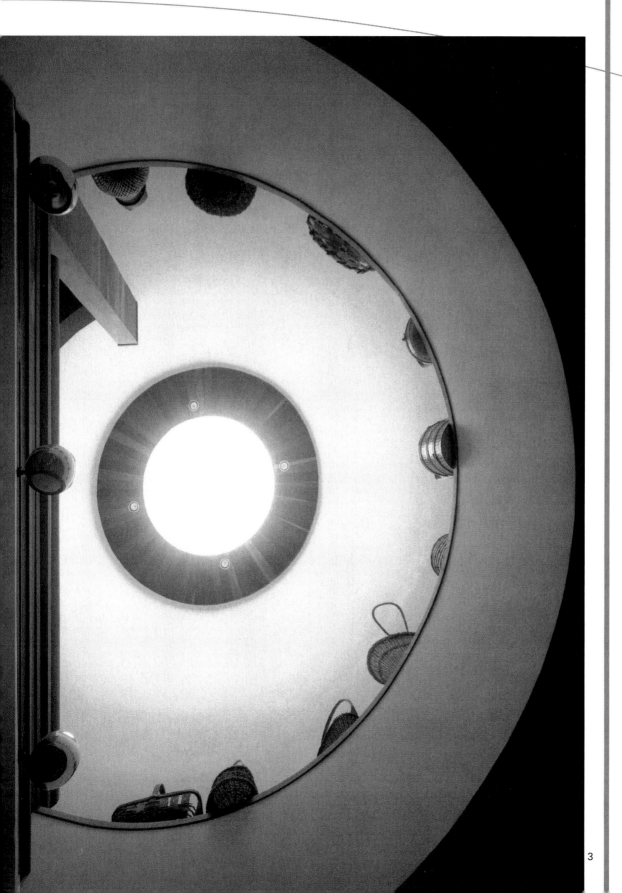

3   The skylit library
4   Silos recall American
    farm vernacular

This home was also an experiment in early hydronic-solar technology. The major design challenge was to develop an energy-efficient home that proved both active and passive solar energy systems could be incorporated as architecturally pleasing forms. Passive solar collection made certain areas, particularly on the south-facing walls, desirable destinations on cooler days. Acting as a passive solar sink, the thermal mass brick flooring in the solarium retained heat, while thermostat-controlled top-hinged panels overhead allowed ventilation to circulate through the house.

4

Suspended lofts created interesting over-looks to the lower floor planes. The residence was defined with adult and children's territories as well as flexible spaces that connected the family area and garage by a sliding interior barn door, enlarging the entertainment areas.

Organic shapes in this structure were clad in redwood and punctuated with brick. Roof shapes radiating from the pivotal silos sloped to the surrounding grades, creating a low peripheral silhouette. The entire house became a wood sculpture blending into the natural forms of the garden, encouraging human interplay and response.

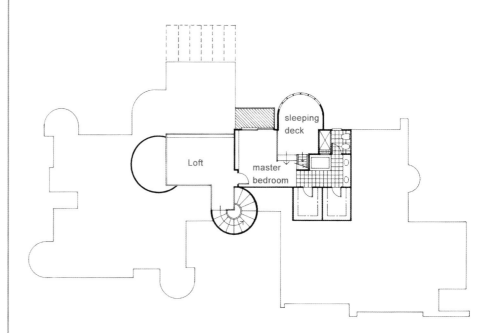

7

Quite often, architecture that breaks from convention or tradition is at risk of being misinterpreted and physically altered by future residents. Such was the case with Via Vistosa. Although several subsequent owners carefully cared for and appreciated this home, one chose to convert the color scheme to suggest a Victorian character by covering the natural redwood with white and blue paint. This visual alteration strongly compromised the original intention of the design, and the richness of the building disappeared. As it was transferred to yet another owner, it was demolished.

As an architect who is willing to venture from the known path, I believe you must develop a mental detachment from many of your works, and move on. Via Vistosa lives in its photographs, in historical books of this region, and as an ephemeral piece in my mind—a schooling block—with fond memories.

5   Master bedroom with loft
6   Main hall and stair
7   Solar panels provide an
    alternative energy source

via abrigada and art box

1985 | santa barbara, california

The organic and geometric forms that were at play in Via Vistosa further evolved in the design of Via Abrigada. Situated on a south-facing ridge overlooking the Pacific Ocean, the home's sculpted horizontal and vertical planes reference billowing spinnakers on a distant ocean horizon. Outlines of a sail are reflected in dormer vaults, which break the linear roof pattern.

1

1 Rear view of Via Abrigada from the sculpture garden. Calder's *Dragon* is in the foreground
2 A Fletcher Benton sculpture mirrors the curve of Abrigada's dormer windows

2

3

A primary design challenge was to build upon the extraordinary ocean and mountain views, while providing broad wall surfaces to accommodate large works of art—a balance accomplished through the use of light, proportion, and placement of architectural form. Walls and surfaces were proportionately designed to encompass large-scale works, while uncomplicated detailing and a subtle color palette allowed the interior to serve as a backdrop not in conflict with the art. Horizontal and vertical planes punctuate the art walls and give distinction to each living area.

Structure becomes sculpture in this home. The interior is a three-dimensional landscape punctuated by level changes in the floor and ceiling, breaking up the large interior volumes into intimate spaces. Cantilevered balconies add to the character by introducing the idea of a village with overviews of the main street, creating an opportunity to look below. Streets are represented by galleries and corridors connecting sleeping chambers and public spaces.

A compositional balance exists between the home's public and private functions. Public living spaces flow into one another. The master suite and upstairs bedrooms can be closed off from the main body of the house for privacy, while a separate guesthouse accommodates visitors.

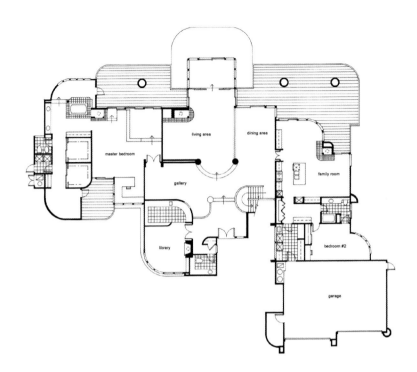

3   The main hall gallery
4   The stair and art lofts

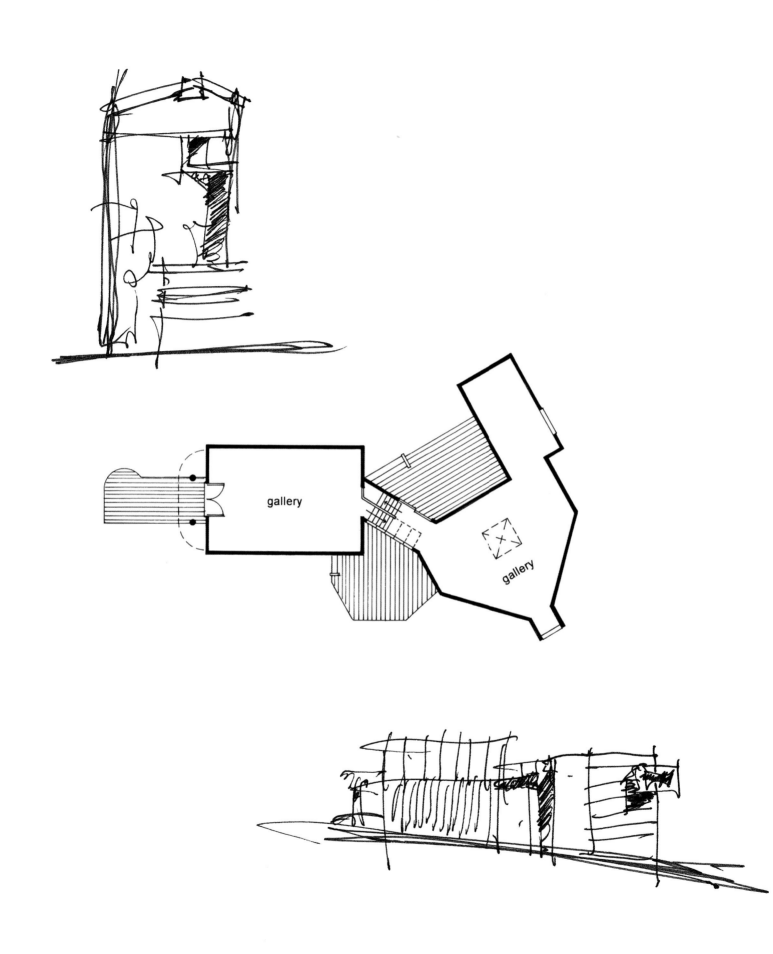

gallery

gallery

Opposite
    A passageway inside the Art Box
Following pages
    Aerial view of the Art Box

The Art Box is an architectural folly in the garden of Via Abrigada where form does not necessarily follow function. Lying on its side, the roof becomes a wall, the chimney acts as a window, and the window becomes a skylight. This toppled art gallery was designed to pay homage to the earthquake Gods in hopes of protecting the art within from future seismic activity prevalent in this area.

schoor residence

1

Comprising a series of gables and bays, the Schoor residence recalls the architecture of traditional English Manor houses. The prominent hillside location in the countryside of Colt's Neck, New Jersey overlooked the owner's equestrian facilities, evoking the regional vernacular of English country estates.

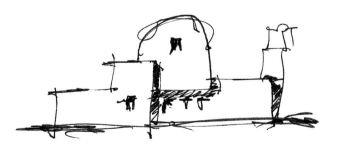

1   The pool house
2   Aerial view of the Schoor residence
    and pool house

46

2

3 Sitting bay
4 A bridge entry connects to informal
   living areas
5 A pastoral landscape surrounds the
   hilltop Schoor residence

3

4

Interior designer Carey Berkus worked with the clients to achieve a light and pleasant environment within the house. Spatial relationships were sculpted to function as an interior landscape to provide uplifting experiences, even during the grayest parts of the year, by utilizing the passage of light through openings and controlled fenestration. Ample exterior glazing allows internal illumination, minimizing the sensation of containment during the colder seasons and providing a profusion of light. High walls throughout the interior supply surface areas for art. Volume and shape within the open floor plan are separated with platforms connected by bridges and passageways, joining the open living areas. Private niches complement the open spaces, adding to an environment with formal and informal destinations.

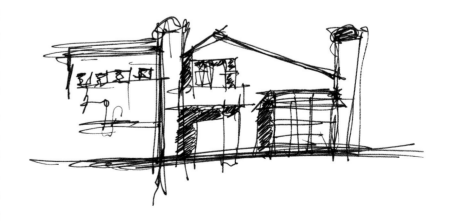

7

6   Interior stair
7   Overlooks from bridge and loft
Opposite
    Formal living area

9

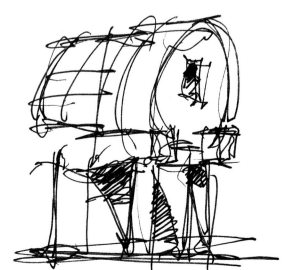

Tropical colors and shapes incorporated in the adjacent pool house conjure visions
vacation retreat off the eastern seaboard. This play of color and form mitigates
desolate landscape of the winter months by creating a visual retreat from the eleme
The form incorporated in the pool house is a structural allusion to a stallion on the h
tribute to the client's interest in standard bred horses. The main barrel vault represe
the body of the horse, with the appendages making reference to the balance of equ
anatomy.

10

11

9 View from pool
10 Cabana entrance
11 Detail of canopy

siegel residence

Inspired by the Florida coast of Boca Raton, the Siegel residence takes its color cues from the clouds floating over the landscape. The formal geometric design of the structure, in keeping with the needs expressed by the clients, is a marked departure from organic elements of homes I previously designed.

1 Geometric forms and a motorcourt mark the entry
2 Entry of the Siegel residence

1

2

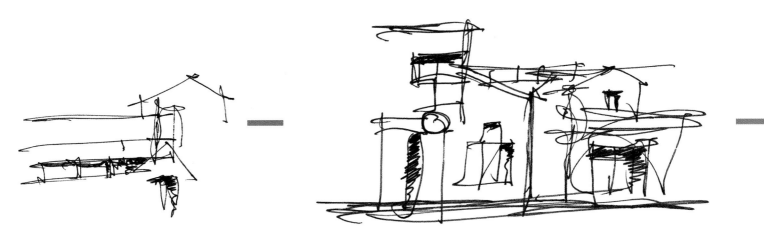

3

3 Motorcourt
4 Hard edges are
 juxtaposed with
 curved surfaces

4

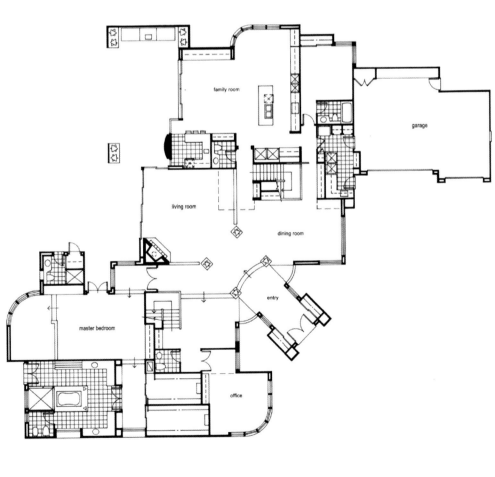

Detail and design continuity were achieved through close collaboration with the client and interior designer Carey Berkus. The resulting structure created a backdrop for art and everyday life patterns. A spatial floor plan and abundant wall space provided a blank canvas for the interior living environs, while alcoves and niches contributed to a dynamic background for the clients' art collection. Bold geometric shapes form partial walls, creating partitions and surfaces for art within the open floor plan without compromising volumetric space. Children's quarters are separate from more formal gathering areas, endowing younger family members with a sense of ownership.

The center pavilion in the house is capped by a steel form representing a ceiling fan, which creates a structural collar tie for the upper roof. Following the roofline, a ribbon of clerestory windows illuminates the house with the movement of clouds and the changing light of day.

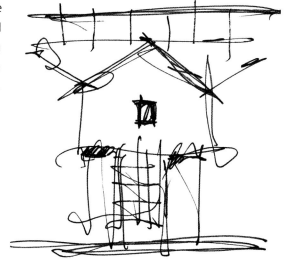

5   Triangle, pyramid, and column marry classical and modernist tradition

Opposite
Purity of color and formal geometry allow the art to speak within the architectural forms

westen residence

montecito, california

One of the closest collaborations during my career was that of working with the Westen family in designing their home in Montecito, California. Though steeped in traditional architecture, Montecito also harbors many contemporary residential structures, including this residence, which is a continuation of the organic series of redwood homes I designed. Conceptualized as a visually and physically engaging organic structure, the house presents new experiences around every turn. As in Via Vistosa, this home again depicts the taming of chaos through the orchestration of forms that do not necessarily fit within a defined design context.

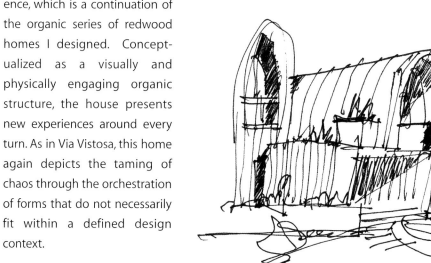

1   Barrel vaults and a highly
    sculpted plane define the
    Westen residence
Opposite
    The vaulted entry

1

As part of the design process, each family member shared his or her perceptions of an ideal living environment, describing spaces that would be stimulating yet practical and livable. The family's three children contributed notes and drawings of how their personal spaces would function within the house. Including the children in the design process stimulated their creativity and validated their importance in the composition of the house.

The Westens' high level of intellectual energy was inspirational for me. As a result, the core of the home was designed as a metaphorical collector of thoughts—similar in concept to a nuclear chamber where particles within collide and separate in a chain reaction—issuing energy. All activities radiated from this central area, which became the spine of the home. The vertical pathway of the staircase offers balconies and semi-circle overlooks compelling one to pause and review the planes below.

3 The living room with cantilevered balconies
4 Stairs and balcony to upper level

4

6

The introduction of light was a major factor in articulating this structure. South-facing walls create a changing environment that allows the house to follow the sun's transition throughout the day. Diversity in fenestration, including windowed vaults and towers, skylights, clerestory windows, and sliding glass doors all create natural illumination. Interior lighting is strategically placed to create an equally diverse landscape at night.

Presenting an amalgamation of light, shadow, and architectural form, the home nourishes the intellectual energy of those within. Hopefully it will leave a legacy of form for those that follow.

5   Entry and elevated sculptural platform
6   The "oval office"
Opposite
     Towers and curves silhouetted by the evening sky

macdonald residence

montecito, california

1

Many of our clients have taken bold leaps of faith by venturing from tried and true vernaculars to explore new architectural relationships and patterns. The MacDonalds were exceptional clients in this regard. Mr. MacDonald wanted to break away from the past, having lived in traditionally styled homes for many years. While Mr. MacDonald was at a time in his life when most people seek familiarity and predictability, he was ready to embark upon an entirely new living experience. I feel architecture can inspire youth and stimulate the mind of those within by introducing interior landscapes that present new impressions each time viewed. I believe Mr. MacDonald shared this philosophy.

The clients' broad philanthropic interests as well as their frequent interaction with extended family meant the home had to serve several functions. We engaged in hours of conversation about their perceptions of space and life patterns. I visited the site to assess view planes and solar orientation.

1 Rear elevation of MacDonald residence
2 Site plan

We came up with the concept of a series of connected pavilions with private chambers linked to gathering areas. This layout enabled the structure to capture a diversity of views from the Pacific Ocean to the surrounding mountain backdrop, while creatively dividing public and private spaces. Guest retreats located on the second floor functioned as isolated getaways. The clients' desire for separate sleeping areas was the impetus for including moving walls in the master bedroom, allowing separation or connection upon demand.

Although this building was never realized, I believe the design of the MacDonald residence would have been a successful living space combining varying geometric forms that many years later had great influence on the conceptual thought process expressed in the Ortega Ridge residence, featured later in this book.

3

3 Front elevation of
  MacDonald residence

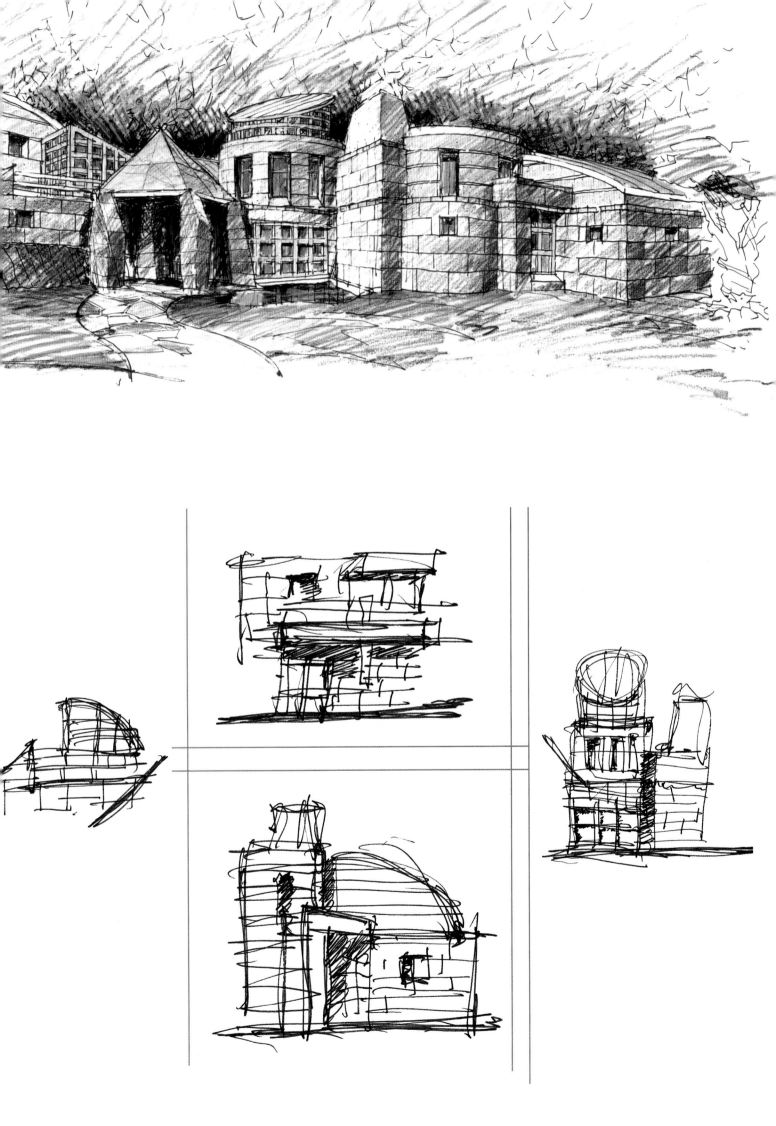

private residence

A continuing interest of mine is to translate our custom home design experience to homes designed for people I may never meet. This residence as well as the following private residence (pages 74–77) were originally designed to respond to a for-sale niche market of one-of-a-kind luxury homes in Palm Desert, California.

Without a specific client in mind, components needed to be crafted to form a logical pattern of uses that appeal to more than one individual. Custom homes frequently present bold gestures in form and pattern—they are designed to be unique, fashioned around the personality of the client. When designing for an unknown occupant, these forms tend to be much more neutral.

Many traditional homes are designed as a series of compartments and barriers. The visitor is asked to pause and await an invitation to enter the interior spaces of the home. I believe a home should present a more approachable environment. This can be accomplished upon first contact by the arrangement of the spatial diagramming. Many of my designs immediately invite one to be a part of the celebration of space by letting the eye move through glazed walls to the areas beyond, summoning forward movement and exploration of the interior spatial relationships. This is particularly true in this residence, whereupon entering the home, the visitor is immediately presented with open views to the interior environment as well as the surrounding exterior landscape.

1   The structure's forms and colors meld
    with the desert landscape
Opposite
    Procession through entry courtyard

1

Like others in this series, the house is associated with golf and open greenways, visually extending the built environment in contrast to the surrounding desert landscape. Set against a backdrop of sloping hills covered with chaparral, the structure blends into the sparse terrain with an undulating roofline and muted earth tones, paying homage to the desert.

A columned arcade leads to a prominent entryway referencing components of the early architectural style of Frank Lloyd Wright. A platform bridge spans the pond and leads to the main entrance, which becomes the focal point of the structure. The central hall is an axial shape providing a hub from which other areas radiate. Interior living areas are capped by varying ceiling planes including angled geometric shapes and the softer form of the oval, reflecting the mountain and landscape formations outside. One of the most interesting aspects of this structure is a raised oval roof form set upon an illuminated wall of glass, giving special distinction to the areas below.

Covered porticos along the passive side of the structure follow the line of the adjacent water feature, creating areas of repose that offer refuge from the high desert sun. The finished home structurally defers to its desert environs while presenting an experience that is stimulating yet serene.

3

3 View of mountains from living room
4 Surrounding rock formations and vegetation inspired the home's color palette

private residence

This home was initially designed for a developer in Palm Desert, California. While this residence incorporates spaces and principles that would appeal to a larger audience, it stands out as a unique piece of architecture amongst a series of luxury homes.

We took creative liberty with this design by introducing a distinctive overhead copper form at the entry. This circular form references the celestial nature of that above, while presenting a shape that is strongly associated with security and bonding. The resulting overhead form adds strength within the facade of this home, presenting an atypical shape that has become a reference point as you pass through this community. Viga pole columns supporting this structure speak to the southwest origins of desert architecture, while water flowing into a small pond within the entryway conveys the idea of home as an oasis within the desert.

1 Spherical copper form at entry
2 Entry court
3 The living room's circular element from the pool

1

2

4   The living room is illuminated by clerestory windows
5   Views of the golf course from the kitchen

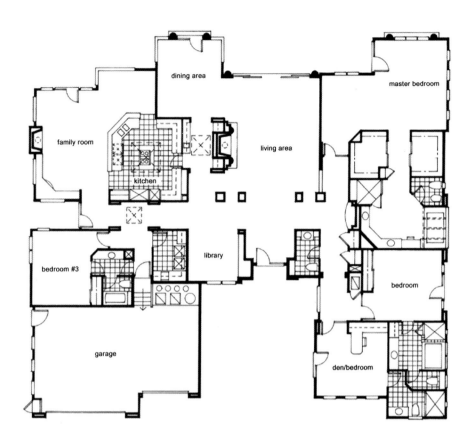

The interior environment of the residence segues from room to room with marked differences in ceiling planes. Clerestory glass protected by copper hoods allows the eye to view the distant mountains and skyline, punctuating the exterior envelope in a sculptural fashion. More intimate nooks and sitting areas offset large dining, living, and family rooms oriented to capture views of the golf course and immediate surroundings. Located to the left of the entryway, a gallery and library provide additional areas for reflection and solitude.

One highly rewarding aspect of being an architect is the chance to continue learning, translating, and dreaming for others. Whether designing for a known or unknown occupant, my goal is to create an architectural experience that sparks an affinity between the individual or family and the structure. I believe this residence successfully achieves this goal.

henry residence

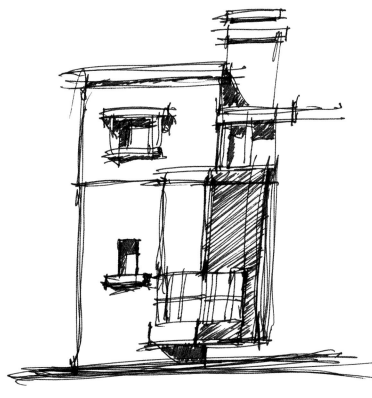

Physical, visual, and historical aspects of the site and its location heavily influenced the design of the Henry house. The site required that the house be built in an angled form, respecting the surrounding trees and canyon. Existing historical architecture in the area created by Frank Lloyd Wright and Greene and Greene meant the house had to truly respect the architectural history of place. Set between two historic bridges spanning an arroyo in Pasadena, California, the house evolved as a series of bridges and sentinels holding their positions among the existing bridges.

1   Columns mark the entry of the residence
Opposite
    Exterior form of the cantilevered library

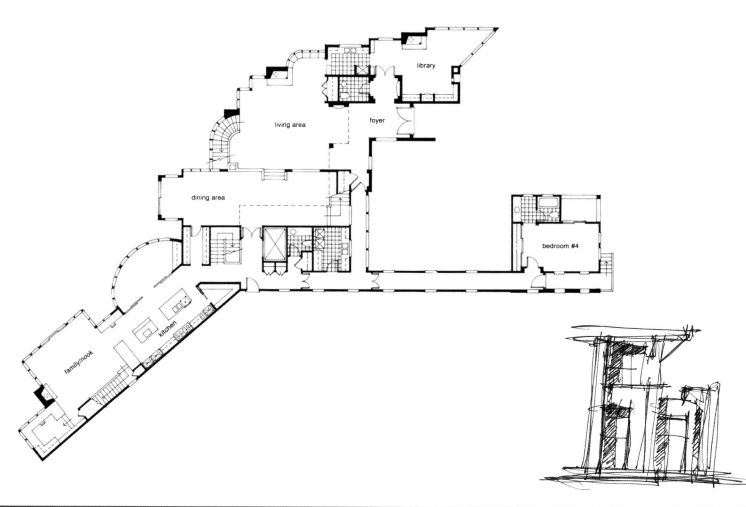

library

living area

foyer

dining area

bedroom #4

kitchen

family/nook

The Henrys looked at sites that would remove them from the urban fabric of the city and place them in a more secluded, natural landscape without compromising their current social and cultural lifestyles. Designed to accommodate the flow of entertainment, as well as operatic and orchestral music, this house is a strong example of sculpting architectural form around human activity. Structurally, it is a performance piece, a stage for people to gather and display their cultural talents.

At the same time, the bridged walkways on the upper levels lead to areas of personal retreat, and architecturally sculpted spaces, such as the library, offer destinations for reflection.

4

Opposite
    Outdoor patios and walkways create
    platforms for entertaining guests
4   Stairway to living areas

The library is designed as a prow of a ship cantilevered over the water, which became one of the primary concepts in the patterning of this home. Spatial relationships created between the inhabitants and the structure of the library produce an atmosphere of contemplation. Located in proximity to the entry bridge, the library seems to float over the reflective pond. Low viewing windows, inspired by stays in Japan, are set below eye level. Their placement begs one to sit to fully comprehend the exterior landscape. The request to rest is done in both a subliminal and literal manner.

5 The outdoor landscape becomes the focal point in the library
6 Interior columns mirror abutments on the bridge outside

5

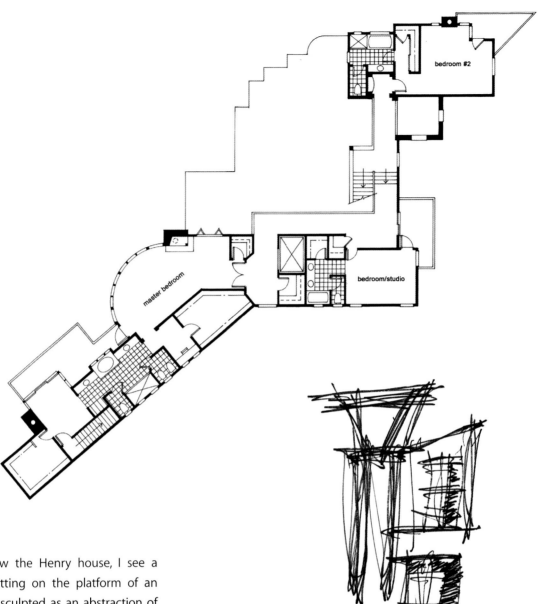

When I view the Henry house, I see a sculpture sitting on the platform of an arroyo. It is sculpted as an abstraction of bridges that surround the site. The entrance sequence begins by entering over a bridge bordered by a colonnade of sentinels. Second floor pathways, which open to the volumetric space of the first floor, become overlooks. Two-story supportive columns mirror the columns of the distant bridge form, while becoming points of definition within the living space. The structure overlooking the arroyo presents a continuum of adjacent organic and geometric shapes, reminiscent of patterns found in the bridges to the north and south. This continuity between the exterior and interior environment guides movement throughout and bonds the home to the site.

terner residence

| pacific palisades, california

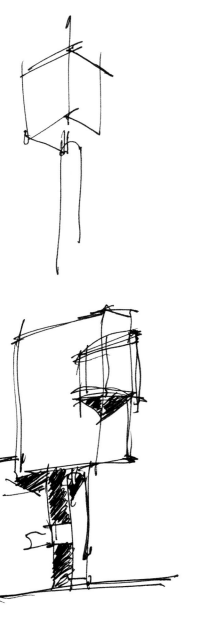

The Terner residence presented an extraordinary opportunity: the chance to restore a piece of architectural history and design a new contemporary residence. Initially, the Terners enlisted my help to choose a site for the contemporary home they had envisioned. When I saw the Pacific Palisades site, I knew it was an ideal palette for the kind of house the clients desired. As well, the site offered the exciting challenge of revitalizing Case Study House #9, a modernist structure designed by Charles Eames and Eero Saarinen. Commissioned by John Entenza in the late 1940s as part of *Arts and Architecture* magazine's Case Study House program, this house was designed to display the best technological and industrial innovations of the time, while providing a flexible alternative to postwar tract developments.

The challenge of this project was determining how to extend modernism beyond the decades of the 1940s and 1950s, while designing a new home that would not conflict with the simple lines and angularity of the Entenza house.

1   A juxtaposition of old and new; the restored
    Case Study House #9 and the newly built
    Terner Residence

1

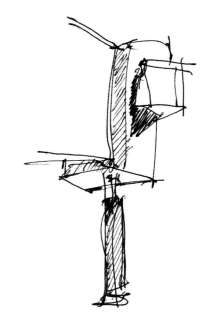

2

3

It was my desire as an architect to implement a new paradigm in modernism that referenced cubism. The triangular windows, sculpted in the image of a Picasso or Braque, became the eyes of the house.

A steel pin and column combination presents a more slender and fragile interpretation of the classical column form, an idea that originated as an abstract of LeCorbusier's modernist Villa Savoye in France.

5

ch cubed form on the exterior, color coded in subtle hues, is an chitectural sculpture interwoven with modernist and ntemporary design.

2–5   Exterior of Terner residence
Following pages
      Terner residence and remodeled
      Entenza house (left side)

Reflecting the clients' love of art, the new house emerged as a cubist piece, a placeholder in the garden juxtaposing the renovated modernist house. I connected the original Entenza house to the Terner house with a delicate blade, delineating two unique pieces of architecture in harmony with one another.

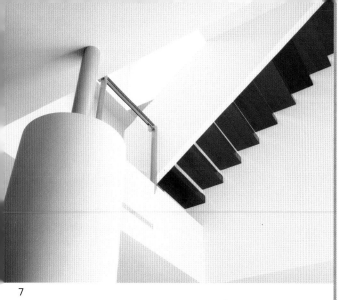

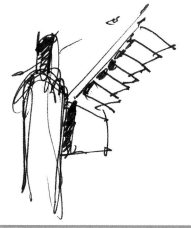

The interior of the Terner residence was designed to be flexible for both formal social engagements and informal events. Shoji screens throughout the home provide opportunities to change spatial patterns within. The careful placement of art and interior lighting reflects the connection between sculpted space, thought, and feeling. Hallways connect private chambers and more public areas.

The vertical element in the center, which houses Mrs. Terner's office, delineates the interior space. Like a watchtower in a village, her third-floor office becomes the center of control.

The Terner's contemporary art collection and intellectual pursuits are mirrored in the articulate lines and angles in the built form of this home. The entire structure provides a backdrop for artistic display and expression, allowing the occupants to emerge as important players within the context of the architecture.

7   Exterior elements such as the steel pin columns are mirrored
    throughout the structure
8   Flexible space is possible by sliding Shoji screens
Opposite
    Interiors by Dana Berkus

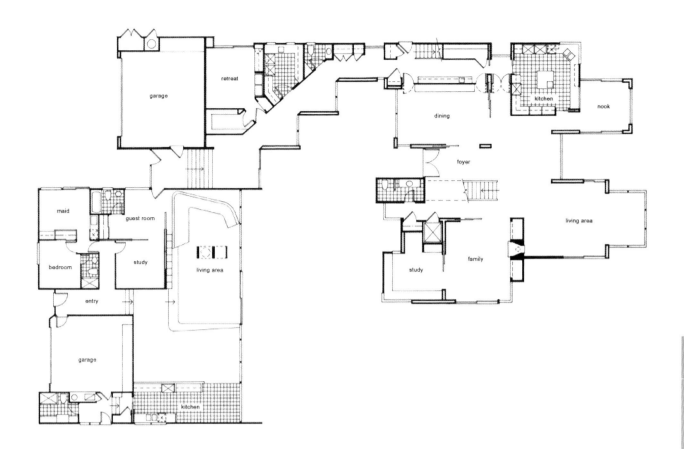

garage

retreat

kitchen

nook

dining

foyer

maid

guest room

living area

study

living area

bedroom

study

family

entry

garage

kitchen

10   Furniture and art complement the spatial planes

11

11 Mid-century modern
furniture is consistent with
the era in which the Case
Study house was originally
designed

12 Eames inspired colors and
geometry mark the
entrance

13 Exterior elevations were
restored to their original
textures and colors

The renovation of the Entenza house paid tribute to its modernist roots as a "bachelor-pad", re-emerging as a guest-house. Certain elements were diligently restored to be as close to their original condition as possible. A contemporary interpretation was applied to other elements. The resulting creation is a testament to the modernist era, as well as a complementary counterpart to the new Terner residence.

weekley residence

1997 | carmel, california

Built as a vacation retreat on a rock ledge of the Pacific coast of California, this structure takes its architectural clues from the Hamptons and other seaside communities on the eastern seaboard. From an aerial view, the copper and slate roofs resemble leaves floating above the rocks. Viewed from a distance, the house appears as a series of linked cottages with a combination of gables and vaults making each destination a unique retreat.

Due to the high visibility of this site location, neighbors became concerned that this new structure would obstruct their views. In order to alleviate their anxiety, they were invited to become part of the design process by delineating the view planes they were interested in saving. The responsibility of the architect was to facilitate this interaction by ensuring that the house fit within the delineated boundaries without interrupting the views of the rocks beyond.

1   The Weekley residence follows the jagged coastline

1

2

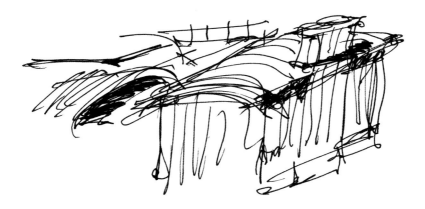

2 The ocean's influence is seen in the curve of the
   copper roof forms and;
3 in the design of the armature of an outdoor light
4 Slate and copper roofs recall the billowing form
   of a ship's sail

3

Secondary homes are often designed to form a distinctive experience not possible in a primary residence. The Weekleys desired a structure that would convey a relaxed attitude to accommodate family vacations, getaways with friends, and corporate retreats in a stimulating, natural environment. Private suites and destinations within the home, connected by passages, reflect this purpose by imparting a sense of privacy and seclusion.

Physically and visually interacting with the seascape, the Weekley house creates the sensation of being on the sea. The main living space is sculpted as a ship's cabin with oak plank curved ceilings over the main living area. Hour to hour, the environment changes—weather patterns threatening and dark, other times calm. The personality of the house changes radically with the light, presenting the inhabitants with a dynamic exchange with the natural environment while offering protection from the elements.

The owners are intently aware and respectful of natural cycles, and the layout of this residence is sculpted inside and out to match this intent. The multiple-level design of the house moves with the rock formations in the rugged landscape, stepping up and down the cliff. View planes, designed to look down into the inlets and coves of the Pacific, absorb the ocean's beauty and inspiration as well as its undeniable power.

Opposite
  Indigenous stone weds the structure to the rugged
  promontory
6 Polished woodwork is reminiscent of a finely crafted
  ship's cabin

yagoda residence

| scottsdale, arizona

1

Although the conceptual design of a custom home is usually developed over a period of time through multiple conversations and collaborative sessions with the client, the skeletal form for the Yagoda residence was accomplished in the first sitting. The completed project looks very much like our first schematics. The clients' clear articulation of their program allowed initial thoughts to flow freely from mind to hand in sketch format.

The resulting residence is designed around a series of interior and exterior courtyards structurally conceived to bring the desert landscape into the home. Located in a community north of Scottsdale, Arizona, the structure's silhouette is an interplay of rectangular forms, each building upon the other, recalling the architectural forms found in high desert pueblo enclaves. Acting as a hinge, a pivotal circular form anchors the dwelling. Similar to a clock tower in a town square, this shape is the centerpiece from which the series of forms emanates.

1   Flat roof design with
    punctuated forms creates
    balance between man-made
    and desert environs

2

Unobstructed viewplanes, sun angle, and privacy were essential factors in determining the physical orientation of the site. A protective wall buffers exterior influences while delineating a boundary between the structure and its surrounding environs. Columns along the outside path create direction and stand squarely like sentinels, leading to the entry. Two-story glass walls create open views of geological outcroppings and the distant city beyond.

2 Columns mark the entry
3 Clerestory elements allow natural light
  to fill the home
Opposite
  Architectural elements maximize
  views and natural light

3

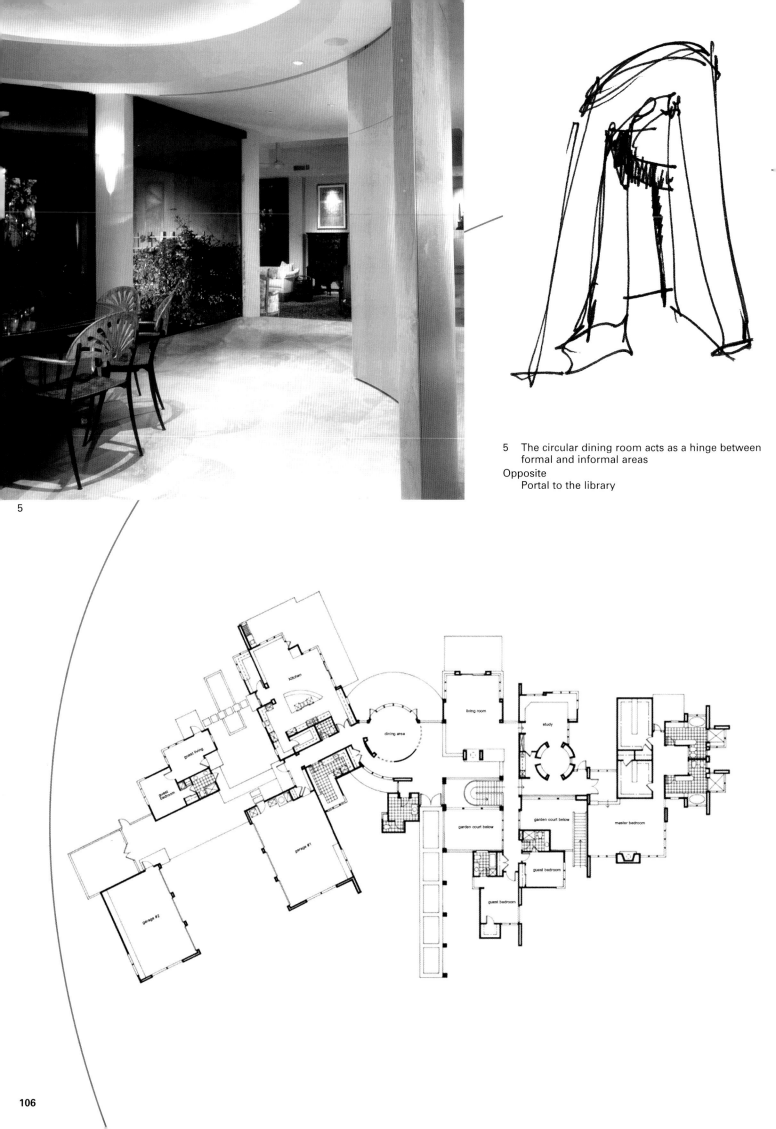

5 The circular dining room acts as a hinge between formal and informal areas
Opposite
Portal to the library

Kitchen

guest living

guest bedroom

garage #1

garage #2

dining area

living room

study

garden court below

garden court below

master bedroom

guest bedroom

guest bedroom

Creating an ambiance of tranquility, the interior of the home is carved to accommodate day-to-day life functions as well as social events by a series of linked living areas radiating from the circular dining area. An interior passageway forms a bridge overlooking sunken gardens. Large wall planes and sculptural niches were designed in response to the clients' passion for art. The strong colors and the conical shape of the library present an interesting focal point off the main circulation corridor. This cylindrical room contains books and seating, and acts as a segue from the passageway to the inner office.

Today, when I speak with the Yagodas, they say if given the opportunity to design their home anew, they would not make a single alteration. It is very rewarding to see clients who were excited and stimulated by the design of their home continue to be engaged with their creation as time passes.

Opposite
A staircase descends through the volume space of the interior sunken courtyard

private residence

palm desert, california

Commissioned by a couple from Tennessee, this home evolved as a structure in contrast to the traditional surroundings of their primary residence. Out of all the houses I've designed, this is one of the most sculptural in its plan form. The geometry of the house creates unique destinations within, evoking the sensation one is on a journey. The arch of the main passageway running the length of the house is similar to a curved walkway through a village; it becomes the linking element, offering a series of hidden destinations to be discovered while introducing the element of surprise.

Located in a California desert community, the residence is situated on a junction of golf fairways—a stark contrast to the natural desert backdrop. A curved progression of monolithic forms crosses the entry walk, creating a transition between the surrounding environment and the home. Landscape walls mirror the contours of the house, sometimes curved, other times angular, visually delineating the perimeter.

A fluid relationship between indoor and outdoor planes reflects the ability to move freely inside and out during different times of the year. The outside fireplaces and seating spaces encourage movement and uses beyond the interior borders of the space while living functions within the home are oriented to immediate and distant viewscapes. An elevated roof terrace overlooks the dramatic desert setting.

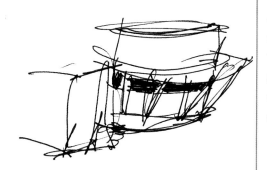

1   Computer rendering of residence
2   Model with view of entry courtyard

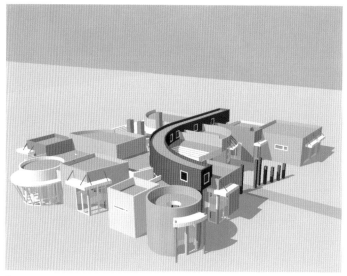

1

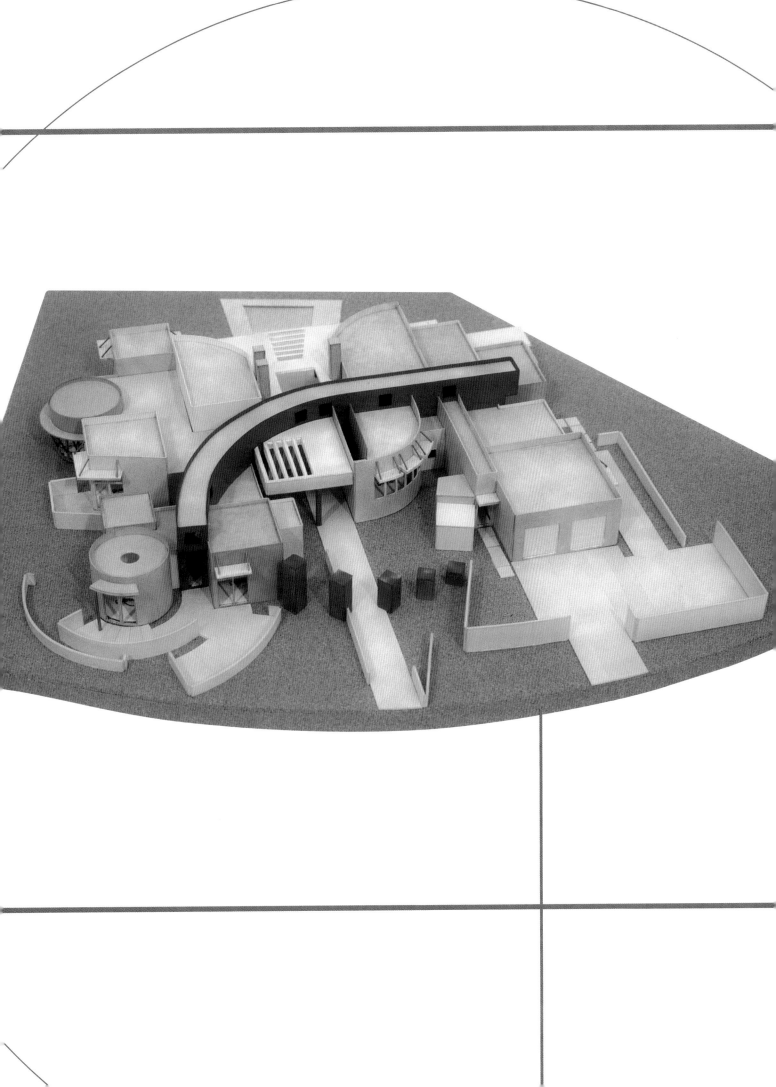

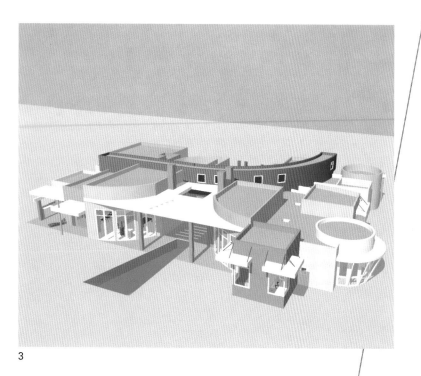

3

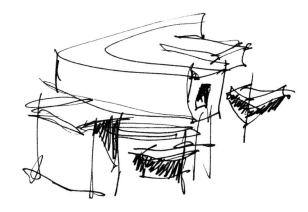

3 Computer rendering
4 Rear elevation shown by model

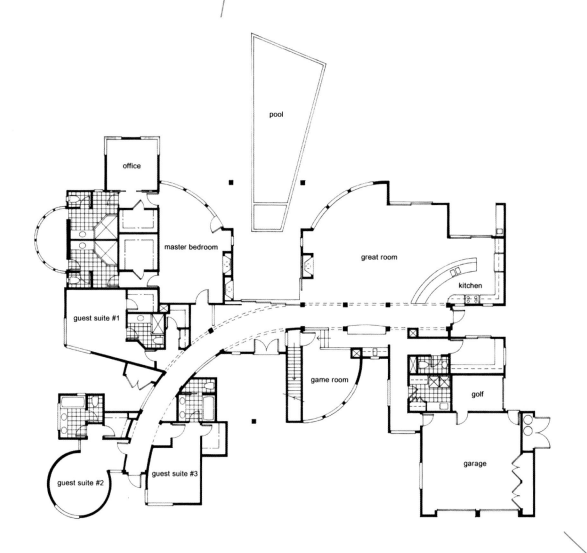

pool

office

master bedroom

great room

kitchen

guest suite #1

game room

golf

guest suite #2

guest suite #3

garage

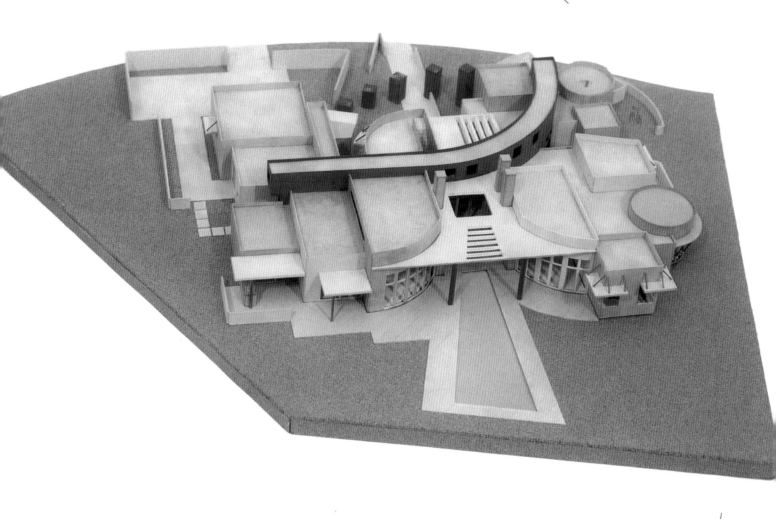

Each destination is architecturally sculpted to be unique. A circular room is introduced at the home's edge, providing a soft and inviting form at the entry to the residence. Trapezoidal, circular, and rectangular in shape, the guest rooms offer different experiences. The home's open plan encourages interaction and activity.

ortega ridge residence

2002 | summerland, california

1

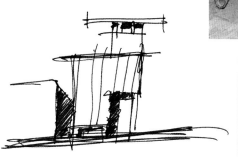

Exterior shapes and forms meld with the surrounding landscape of this hilltop residence. Commissioned by a European couple desiring a retreat in Santa Barbara, the home is intended as a destination in which to relax and one that conveys a spirit of harmony within. A series of blades and organic forms represent the structural landscape.

Block sentinels capped with glass clerestories illuminate the passageways within and punctuate the concrete, steel, and wood structure.

Functioning as a series of pavilions designed around the 360-degree hilltop views, the house contains a high level of fenestration, bringing light and landscape into the home. Each interior space captures a different aspect of the distant landscape. The east-facing master suite is positioned to receive morning light that will engage and illuminate the space. Guest suites located in a separate wing allow zones of privacy for all occupants, while public areas orchestrate a sense of union. Living areas oriented to the southwest are positioned to overlook the swimming pool. Visually, the pool blends with the oceanscape beyond, creating the illusion of two bodies of water merging.

1   Frame of the south facade
2   Computer rendering of south facade

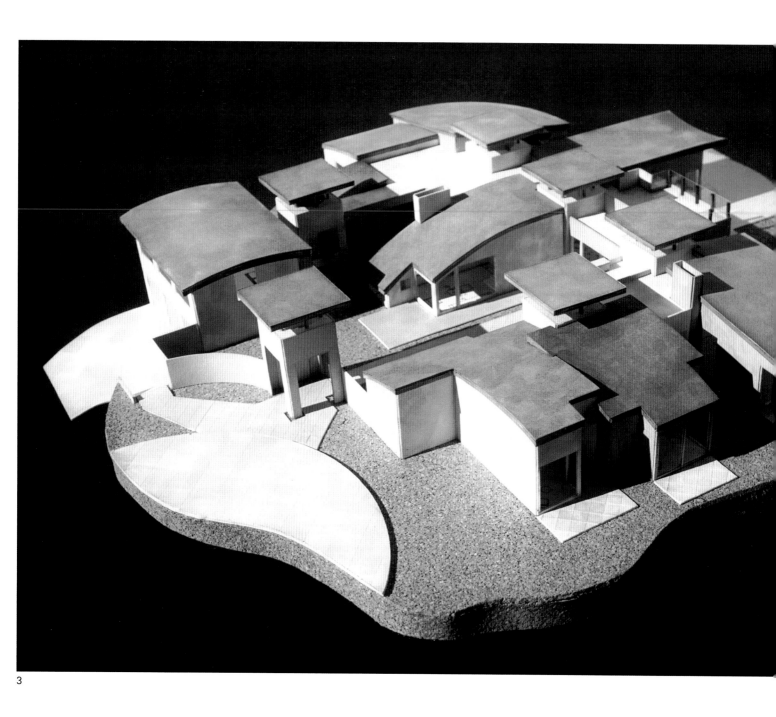

3

Although this site offers ideal viewplanes, it also presented major challenges. The design needed to incorporate the nearly 360-degree views while providing protection from wind gusts on the hilltop site. Embraced by surrounding pavilions, the courtyard is open to sunlight as well as sheltered from the elements.

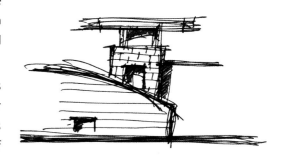

Developing strong lines of communication in the client–architect relationship has always been an essential component in my architectural practice. We often take for granted the ease of communication between people of the same culture. In this particular client–architect relationship, we were presented with the challenge of bridging cultural barriers. I came to understand that the unstated is sometimes as meaningful as the stated. Our working relationship became much more intimate in our efforts to understand the subtleties of meaning. Breakthroughs in communication led to newfound levels of connection and comprehension, making this a valuable and rewarding partnership.

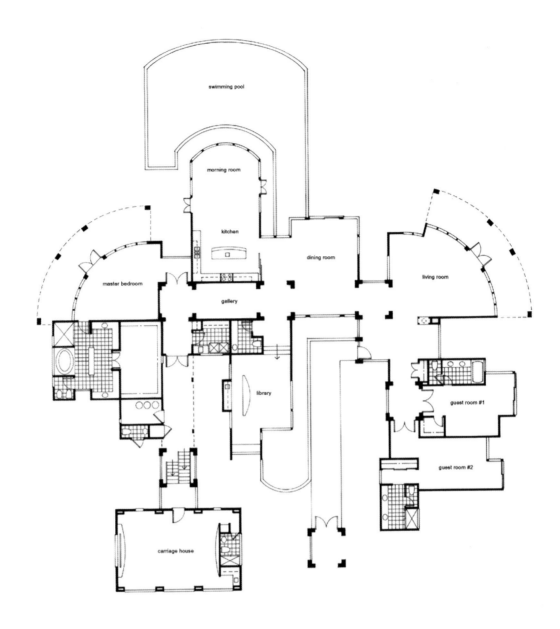

swimming pool

morning room

kitchen

dining room

master bedroom

living room

gallery

library

guest room #1

guest room #2

carriage house

Model
Construction of east
portal

5

5 Computer rendering of courtyard
6 Construction of library
7 Computer rendering of west facade
8 Construction of sentinels

6

7

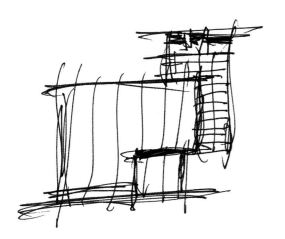

8

conclusion

Each custom home presented in this book provided the highly rewarding experience of interpreting the dreams and aspirations of clients into unique architectural statements. It is my philosophy that shelter is much more than a roof over the occupants' heads. Introducing creative elements such as open floor plans, areas of social interaction, volumes that lift the spirit, and intimate areas of retreat gives us the opportunity to transform nondescript shelters into stimulating personal environments.

I believe that architecture and sculpture play important roles stimulating dialogue between people of diverse backgrounds, contributing to social interaction that may not otherwise take place. On a broad scale, architectural and sculptural icons universally associated with their prospective cities—the Sydney Opera House in Australia, the Eiffel Tower in Paris, the Bilbao Museum in Spain, or Michelangelo's Statue of David in Florence—create a special affiliation for the city and provide common ground for conversation among its residents, regardless of social or economic class.

On a smaller scale, interesting architectural buildings and sculptural pieces within a community can likewise stimulate pride and create backdrops for social interaction by drawing a cross-section of people together. An open marketplace, tower or obelisk, a museum, park, or paseo—all have potential to be a point of social convergence, the "living room" of a community where all are welcome to partake.

It is interesting to contemplate what makes one architectural space engaging and stimulating and another seemingly devoid of human attention. I believe the difference has to do with the creative nature of the crafted space, regardless of architectural vernacular. When sculpted with the intent to stimulate and inspire, a building can become more than just shelter; it can be transformed into a place where people can gather for the good of the community.

Architecture may be viewed as a platform for social integration. When a person enters a creatively sculpted building or public area, he or she is compelled, on some level, to understand the dynamics of that space. This understanding can lead to a shift in perception that often influences the manner in which communication unfolds.

For example, two individuals of different ages or backgrounds may find common ground within a dynamic and intriguing space and may be compelled to interact. Each individual may become a valuable part of the exchange within an environment that may lack social heirarchy. As a society becomes denser, tools of integration and diversity within communities become as important as advances in technology.

In my next written endeavor, I plan to explore the role architecture plays in fostering integration and diversity by investigating the patterns and connections between the microcosm of a single home and the macrocosm of society as a whole. I believe family gatherings around the dining room table play a role as vital in defining a community and its social patterns as interactions in public and open spaces. I am intrigued by the idea of observing the effects stimulating gathering places can have on family and community.

about the author

Founder and President of B3 Architects and Berkus Design Studio, Architect Barry A. Berkus has remained on the forefront of residential design in this country and abroad for over 40 years. Based in Santa Barbara, California, his design and planning practice has had offices in New York, Los Angeles, Irvine, San Francisco, Chicago, Atlanta, Washington, D.C., Miami, and Tokyo. In addition to designing over 60 custom homes, Mr. Berkus has been involved in a broad range of projects including the design of more than 600,000 residences, resort and master-planned communities, urban infill, and commercial and institutional projects. Berkus design teams have received more than 300 design and planning awards from regional, national and international competitions.

Mr. Berkus has been featured in *USA Today, Money, Architectural Record, Progressive Architecture, Art News,* and *Architectural Digest,* which named him one of the world's "Top 100 architects" in 1991. *Professional Builder* honored him as the most innovative architect in the area of housing in the United States. In1999, *Builder* magazine counted Berkus as one of the 100 most influential individuals in the past century of American housing, and the readers of *Residential Architect* selected Berkus as one of the 10 most significant figures of 20th century residential architecture.

Mr. Berkus' influence has not been limited to domestic architecture in the United States. International projects have included the planning of communities in Malaysia and Japan, master-planning of residential villages surrounding EuroDisney in France, and a provincial-government commissioned plan for the redevelopment of the waterfront Expo site in Vancouver, British Columbia.

In the art world, he is equally well known. Mr. Berkus and his late wife Gail Berkus have been named among the world's top 200 art collectors, and he continues to support emerging artists and art institutions. Major museums around the world have shown works from their collection.

Mr. Berkus recently authored *Architecture, Art, Parallels, Connections,* also published by the Images Publishing Group. His own watercolors have been shown at galleries in Santa Barbara and Sun Valley, Idaho. A traveling exhibition including Mr. Berkus' work entitled *Out of Order; Mapping Social Space* traveled to art centers and universities throughout the US in 2001. The exhibit presented a social view of our urban fabric interweaving natural design and technology. Mr. Berkus speaks at universities and symposiums internationally and was one of the keynote speakers for the Urban Land Institute's 50th Anniversary. He has served on the Policy Advisory Board for the Harvard University Joint Center of Housing Studies, and is a current member of the American Institute of Architects and the Urban Land Institute. In 1984, Mr. Berkus served as the Commissioner of Rowing for the Summer Olympic Games in Los Angeles.

Barry A. Berkus, AIA

selected publications

Books:

Architecture, Art, Parallels, Connections, by Barry Berkus,
The Images Publishing Group, Australia 2000;
Watson-Guptill Publishing, New York 2000

Selected publications featuring Mr. Berkus:
Professional Builder, March 2000
Newsday, March 1999
Builder, January 1999
Residential Architect, January 1999
Better Homes and Gardens, November 1998
House and Garden, October 1998
Home, March & June 1998
Newsday, January 1998
San Francisco Examiner, January 1998
Dallas Morning News, January 1998
Newsday, December 1997
Builder, December 1997
Dallas Morning News, October 1997
House Beautiful, October 1997
Home, March 1997
Custom Home, January 1997
Luxury Homes, December 1995
Builder, January 1995
Professional Builder, August 1994
Luxury Homes, April 1994
Architectural Record, January 1994
Better Homes and Gardens, May 1993
Architecture, November 1992
Professional Builder, September 1992
Better Homes and Gardens, May 1992
Custom Home, May 1992
Architectural Digest, August 1991
Popular Science, May 1990
Money, March 1990

Authored articles:

"Architecture for the Unknown." Barry A. Berkus. *Residential Architect,* June 1997, 28–30.
"What is Disney Celebrating?" Barry A. Berkus. *Professional Builder,* September 1996, 49–50.
"Inside Out: Housing Architecture in Evolution." Barry A. Berkus. *Professional Builder,*
 October 1995, 70–78.

Other publications featuring Mr Berkus' work:

Santa Barbara Style. Kathryn Mason, author, with photography by James Chen.
Rizzoli International Publications, Inc. New York, 2001.

Classic modern: midcentury modern at home. Deborah K. Dietsch. Simon & Schuster, New York,
Archetype Press, Inc., 2000.

Out of Order: mapping social space. (Exhibition catalog.) CU Art Galleries, University of Colorado,
Boulder, 2000.

Vertigo: The Strange New World of the Contemporary City. (Exhibition Catalog.) Glasgow
1999: UK City of Architecture and Design, 1999.

Home of the Future Interactive Guide. (CD-ROM.) Builder, Home, Centex Homes, B3
Architects. Hanley-Wood,1998.

Art of the States: Works from a Santa Barbara Collection. (Exhibition catalog.) Robert
McDonald, curator, with foreword by Robert Fitzpatrick. Santa Barbara Museum of Art, 1984.

firm

Berkus Design Studio

Bob Klammer
Benjamin Krintzman
Pat Moser
Cindy Pratt
Keith Rivera
John Rosenfeld
Rand Sisk
Bernard Tamborello
Richard Thorne

B3 Architects

Ellen Adamson
Kristin Anderson
Jason Backhaus
Michael Cervin
Greg Christman
Kim Cornell
Lauren DeChant
Isaac Hendricks
Juun Lee Hwang
Thom McMahon
Pat Moser
Jaime Palencia III
Sylvia Perlee
Stephen Revord
Trish Reynoso
Doug Singletary
Tod H. Stockwell
Eddie Gomes Villaruz
Anne Voorhies
Sherry Willis
August Zamolsky

credits

photography credits

Farshid Assassi 43-45,
Otto Baitz 19, 46 (1), 52-53
Jim Bartsch 78-83
Tom Bonner cover shot, 21 (11), 85, 86, 88-91, 93, 94 (11,12)
Dugan/Powers/Yocum, 60-65
Bob Kohn 32, 33, 35-37
Peter Malinowski 17 (4), 21 (12), 28, 29 (2), 30, 54-55, 56
   with Glenn Cormier, 57-59, 70-73, 74-77, 102-108
Wayne McCall 22, 34
Robb Miller 38-41, 46 (top left), 48-51
Rob Muir 20 (10), 96-97 (1), 100-101
Julius Shulman 29 (3), 31

model credits

Benjamin Krintzman 18 (7), 24 (14), 110, 111, 113,116

computer renderings

Keith Rivera 110, 112, 115, 118, 119

All sketches are by the author, Barry A. Berkus. All architectural
photographs, models and renderings not otherwise cited are
by the author or by employees of the author's affiliated firms
(Barry A. Berkus, AIA; B3 Architects; Berkus Design Studio).
Numbers in parentheses refer to illustration numbers. Numbers not
in parentheses refer to page numbers where the photos cited appear.